Values

Honesty

Kimberley Jane Pryor

Marshall Cavendish
Benchmark
New York

This edition first published in 2009 in the United States of America by Marshall Cavendish Benchmark.

Marshall Cavendish Benchmark
99 White Plains Road
Tarrytown, NY 10591
www.marshallcavendish.us

First published in 2008 by
MACMILLAN EDUCATION AUSTRALIA PTY LTD
15–19 Claremont St, South Yarra 3141

Visit our Web site at www.macmillan.com.au or go directly to www.macmillanlibrary.com.au

Associated companies and representatives throughout the world.

Library of Congress Cataloging-in-Publication Data

Pryor, Kimberley Jane.
    Honesty / by Kimberley Jane Pryor.
        p. cm. — (Values)
    Includes index.
    ISBN 978-0-7614-3125-1
    1. Honesty—Juvenile literature. 2. Children—Conduct of life—Juvenile literature. I. Title.
    BJ1533.H7P79 2008
179'.9—dc22

                                        2008001673

Edited by Helena Newton
Text and cover design by Christine Deering
Page layout by Raul Diche and Domenic Lauricella
Photo research by Naomi Parker and Legend Images

Printed in the United States

Acknowledgments
The author and the publisher are grateful to the following for permission to reproduce copyright material:

Front cover photograph of friends playing a board game © bonnie jacobs/iStockphoto.com

Photos courtesy of:
Corbis RF, 27; Digital Vision, 17; Digital Vision/Getty Images, 14, 20; © Debi Bishop/iStockphoto.com, 10; © Franky De Meyer/iStockphoto.com, 25; © Iiilexmom/iStockphoto.com, 3, 23; © bonnie jacobs/iStockphoto.com, 1, 7, 8; © Erick Jones/iStockphoto.com, 21; © Sean Locke/iStockphoto.com, 26; © Carmen Martínez Banús/iStockphoto.com, 22; © Photoambience/iStockphoto.com, 16; © Alberto Pomares/iStockphoto.com, 5; © Wendy Shiao/iStockphoto.com, 29; © sonyae/iStockphoto.com, 4, 11; © Jamie Wilson/iStockphoto.com, 18; © Lisa F. Young/iStockphoto.com, 28; © Pierre Yu/iStockphoto.com, 6; Photodisc, 9; Photos.com, 12, 13, 19, 24, 30; PureStock, 15.

While every care has been taken to trace and acknowledge copyright, the publisher tenders their apologies for any accidental infringement where copyright has proved untraceable. Where the attempt has been unsuccessful, the publisher welcomes information that would redress the situation.

For Nick, Ashley and Thomas

1 3 5 6 4 2

Contents

Glossary words

When a word is printed in **bold**, you can look up its meaning in the Glossary on page 31.

Values

Values are the things you believe in. They guide the way:

- you think

- you speak

- you **behave**

Values help you play happily with your friends in a playground tunnel.

Values help you to decide what is right and what is wrong. They also help you to live your life in a **meaningful** way.

Values help you to follow the rules of a soccer game.

Honesty

Honesty is telling the truth. It is saying what really happened and telling someone when you make a mistake.

It is honest to admit to breaking a vase.

Honesty is also making sure you do not take things that belong to other people. It is remembering to ask before you **borrow** things from others.

You show honesty when you ask before borrowing a frisbee.

Honest People

Honest people play by the rules of a game.
Sometimes they win and sometimes they lose.
When they win, they win fairly.

Board games are more fun when everyone plays by the rules.

Honest people do not trick others to get what they want. They are trusted by their family, friends, and neighbors.

Honest people do not trick others to get more than their fair share of cookies.

Being Honest with Family

Family members show honesty by saying what they are doing and where they are going. This helps them find each other when they need to.

You show honesty when you ask an adult family member before playing with water.

10

It is honest to tell the truth about who should go next on play equipment. That way everyone is treated fairly.

It is fair to give everyone a turn on the trampoline.

Being Honest with Friends

Friends show honesty when they keep their promises to each other. They know they can trust and **depend** on each other.

Keeping a promise to sit with a friend at lunchtime shows honesty.

Sometimes a friend may leave something at your house. It is honest to give it back, even if your friend has not missed it.

Returning a lost necklace to a friend will make her happy.

Being Honest with Neighbors

People show honesty when they return things that belong to their neighbors. Sometimes people find a toy belonging to a neighbor in their yard.

It is honest to return a toy plane that your neighbor has lost.

Honest people tell the truth to the people in their neighborhood. If a shopkeeper gives them too much change, they say so and give it back.

Honest people return extra change.

Ways To Be Honest

There are many different ways to be honest with your family, friends, and neighbors. Always telling the truth is a good way to start being honest.

If you have not done your homework, it is better to be honest and to tell your teacher.

Making sure that you do not **steal** things is a good way to practice honesty. Keeping the right score is another way to be honest.

Keeping the right score while playing basketball shows honesty.

Telling the Truth

Telling the truth is one way to be honest. When you tell the truth, you make sure something is correct before you say it.

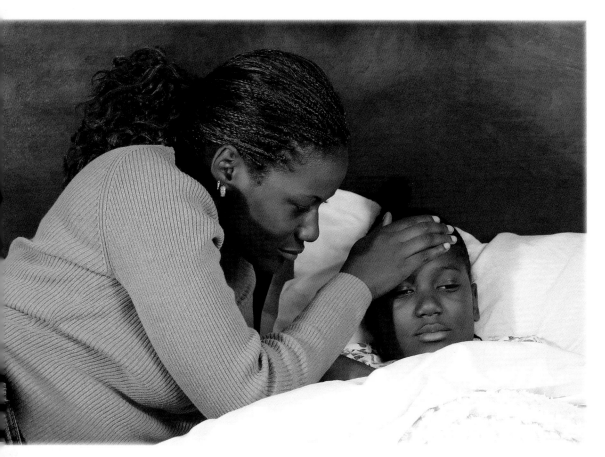

Pretending to feel sick so you can stay at home is not telling the truth.

It is honest to tell the truth about yourself and others. Honest people always tell the truth, even when they are afraid of getting into trouble for doing so.

Honest people admit that they have been mean, even though their teacher will be disappointed.

Not Stealing

Not stealing is another way to be honest.
Honest people do not take things that do not
belong to them.

People feel sad when their belongings are stolen.

Using other people's ideas without **permission** is also stealing. Honest people ask before they use other people's ideas. They say who had the ideas first.

Taking someone else's idea for a story from the Internet is stealing.

Not Cheating

Honest people do not cheat. **Dishonest** people cheat in order to get something, or to do well at something.

Looking at the answers during a test is cheating.

Breaking the rules in order to win a game is also cheating. Honest people follow the rules and have fun whether they win or lose.

Honest people do not cheat at cards.

Being Fair

Part of honesty is being fair. Fair people treat other people **equally**. They do not give more things or more turns to their friends.

It is fair to give everyone a turn at playing with toy cars.

Honest people play fairly. This means they play games by the rules. They do not cry, shout, or complain if they think they are losing.

Fair people do not sulk to get what they want.

Being Trustworthy

Being **trustworthy** is a way to be honest. Trustworthy people do what they say they will do. They do not forget or decide to do something more interesting or important.

Remembering to take notes home from school shows that you are trustworthy.

Trustworthy people can also be trusted to do what others ask them to do. They do not decide to do something else instead.

Eating your healthy lunch from home instead of buying junk food at school shows you can be trusted.

Being Reliable

Being **reliable** is another way to show honesty. Reliable people remember what they have to do and where they have to go. They try not to let others down.

Reliable music students bring their instrument to their weekly lessons.

Reliable people take good care of things that they borrow from others. They also return things that they have borrowed on time.

Librarians rely on people to take good care of the books they borrow from the library.

Personal Set of Values

There are many different values. Everyone has a personal set of values. This set of values guides people in big and little ways in their daily lives.

Honesty is an important value for a judge to have.

Glossary

behave   act in a certain way

borrow   take something for a short time and agree to give it back

depend   feel sure that someone will do the right thing

dishonest   not honest

equally   the same

meaningful   important or valuable

permission   being allowed to

reliable   able to be relied or depended on

steal   take and keep something that does not belong to you

trustworthy   doing what you say you will do

Index